ADVANCE PRAI

D0778041

Wait, What? A Comic Book Guide to Relationships, Bodies, and Growing Up

66 This is the one. This is the book I'll give parents who ask, 'How can I help my kid learn about sex?' The only thing better than sex education that includes everyone is sex education that includes everyone and has a goofy sense of humor. Also, Weird Platypus is my life coach now. 99

- **EMILY NAGOSKI,** sex educator, *New York Times* bestselling author of *Come As You Are*

66 A clear, friendly, informative and inclusive guide for weird platypi & others! 99

- **SARA RYAN,** author of *Empress of the World* and *Bad Houses*

66 Heather Corinna and Isabella Rotman have created the new indispensable classic for kids ready to face down puberty and everything it brings. It offers more than just information about bodies, though — it brings a loving, essential lens to matters of heart and soul, offering a roadmap not only to physical changes, but the complex social and emotional terrain of consent, crushes and identity. 99

- **RABBI DANYA RUTTENBERG,** author of *Nurture the Wow: Finding Spirituality in the Frustration, Boredom, Tears, Poop, Desperation, Wonder, and Radical Amazement of Parenting*

66 This dream team of creators came up with a book that is not only accessible, but totally enjoyable to read! I'm so excited to see *Wait, What?* in every library, school and doctor's office! 99

- **ARCHIE BONGIOVANNI,** co-creator of *A Quick & Easy Guide to They/Them Pronouns*

A LIMERENCE PRESS
PUBLICATION

wait, WHAT?

A Comic Book Guide to Relationships, Bodies, and Growing Up

By

HEATHER CORINNA & ISABELLA ROTMAN

Colored by LUKE B. HOWARD

Designed by Sonja Synak
Edited by Ari Yarwood

Published by Limerence Press

Ari Yarwood,
founder & editorial director

Limerence Press is
an imprint of Oni Press, Inc.

Joe Nozemack,
founder & chief financial officer

James Lucas Jones,
publisher

Sarah Gaydos,
editor in chief

Charlie Chu,
v.p. of creative & business development

Brad Rooks,
director of operations

Melissa Meszaros,
director of publicity

Margot Wood,
director of sales

Sandy Tanaka,
marketing design manager

Amber O'Neill,
special projects manager

Troy Look,
director of design & production

Kate Z. Stone,
senior graphic designer

Sonja Synak,
graphic designer

Angie Knowles,
digital prepress lead

Robin Herrera,
senior editor

Ari Yarwood,
senior editor

Desiree Wilson,
associate editor

Kate Light,
editorial assistant

Michelle Nguyen,
executive assistant

Jung Lee,
logistics coordinator

LIMERENCE
PRESS

1319 SE Martin Luther King, Jr. Blvd.
Suite 240
Portland, OR 97214

limerencepress.com
twitter.com/limerencepress

scarleteen.com
twitter.com/scarleteen
instagram.com/scarleteenorg
hellyeahscarleteen.tumblr.com
facebook.com/Scarleteen

First Edition: September 2019
ISBN: 978-1-62010-659-4
eISBN: 978-1-62010-660-0

1 2 3 4 5 6 7 8 9 10

Library of Congress Control Number: 2019931600

Printed in Hong Kong.

WHAT'S IN
THIS BOOK?

SCARLETEEN
sex ed for the real world

We've made this comic as a get-started guide for a time of life when you or your friends are probably starting to have some new things going on with your bodies, your relationships, your feelings and your sexualities.

A good guide can sure come in handy right about now. Some of these things make a lot of people feel confused, nervous or overwhelmed. We're aiming to help you feel less confused or weirded-out and more confident and chill about all this stuff.

What's inside this book might be all you want or need right now. Some parts of it may even feel like *more* than you want or need. On the other hand, you might find this book gets you wanting to know more, or makes you more curious about sex, bodies or relationships. You might want or need information that isn't in here at all.

We both work at Scarleteen, a sex and relationships information, education and support organization and resource that's mostly made for teenagers and people in their twenties. The website for Scarleteen — **www.scarleteen.com** — has thousands of pages of accurate, thoughtful and inclusive information if you want more than this book offers. Scarleteen also offers direct help and support services, like a mobile helpline you can use by texting us at (206) 866-2279. If you or a friend need a real, live, safe person to talk to about the kinds of things inside this book, Scarleteen can help you out. Heather also wrote (and Isabella also illustrated) the book *S.E.X: The All-You-Need-to-Know Sexuality Guide to Get You Through Your Teens and Twenties*, if and when you're ready for a much bigger book with more advanced knowledge.

Welcome to our lunch table, where we talk about EVERYTHING!

SO WHO'S AT THE LUNCH TABLE?

You can call me Rico. When I moved here, kids just didn't get me, but these guys are cool.

RICO

Hi, I'm Malia! I've known Sam and Max since preschool.

MALIA

I'm Max. I rollerskate every weekend. I play Scrabble competitively. I have two lizards.

MAX

Hi! I'm Sam. Malia and Max and I have been together through everything. I'm so glad Rico and Alexis are here now too.

SAM

Hello, my name is Alexis. My dad's in the army, so I move a lot, but I couldn't have found better friends than this group.

ALEXIS

Due Dates

SOMETIMES IT CAN FEEL LIKE EVERYTHING NEEDS TO HAPPEN AT *a certain time.* IF IT DOESN'T HAPPEN *at that time,* IT CAN SEEM LIKE YOU ARE EITHER TOO LATE OR TOO EARLY. NO ONE EVER SEEMS TO FEEL *right on time.*

Human sexual development and sexuality are very diverse. It's not just one or two different ways for everyone. You know how all of our faces look different? Or how many different ice cream flavors there are? Our bodies and sexualities are some of the most unique things about us. There really are no specific ages, times or other deadlines when someone should be or must be at a certain place with their sexuality or their body.

It sure can feel like there are, though. If it seems like most people around you are already at certain places in their physical development or doing sexual things, you might assume those are the "right" times, not just *their* times. You might think anyone ahead of them is early or behind them is late. But that's wrong and we can really stress ourselves out if we think about it that way. We can even be more likely to make choices that aren't right for us or what we really want.

Some changes aren't a choice, like how bodies change. The right time for your body's changes is just when your body is changing. The right time for things that are a choice — like kissing someone — is when *you* want to and when it feels right for *you* (and anyone else involved!).

WHAT DO YOU THINK AND WHERE ARE YOU AT?

IRL IN REAL LIFE!

THE WAY THINGS ARE IN MEDIA IS NOT NECESSARILY HOW THEY ACTUALLY ARE.

Mass or popular media — that's communication that reaches a lot of people in a short time, like TV, movies or newspapers — is more often fiction than non-fiction, even when the word "reality" is attached or when someone has made the media themselves to teach or explain something. Media "reality" is not reality. Popular media is mostly meant to entertain or advertise, not educate or show real life. It's usually more fantasy than reality.

Some things are very different IRL than they are in movies, TV, videos or other popular media. People in popular media don't often look like people do in real life. Even *they* look different IRL. The same is true for relationships and sex. How those things are shown or talked about in media — including porn — aren't usually how they are for real or good examples of how to do them in ways that are often wanted, healthy or safe in reality.

WHAT IS PUBERTY?

Puberty is a term used to describe the process of development of a body's general shape and size and the maturation of the genitals and the internal reproductive organs.

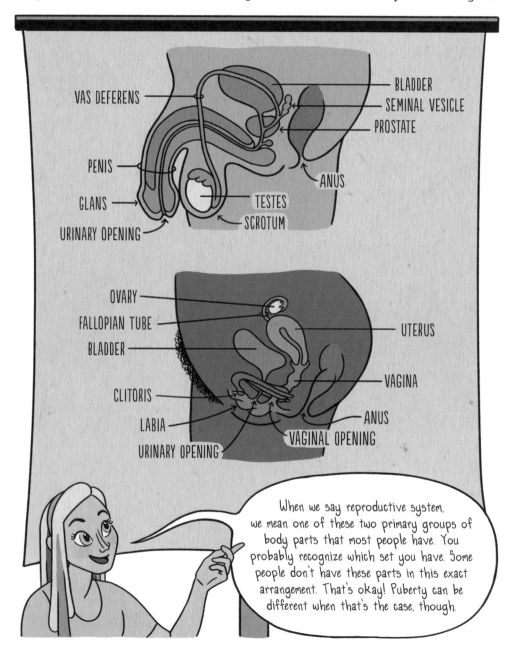

When we say reproductive system, we mean one of these two primary groups of body parts that most people have. You probably recognize which set you have. Some people don't have these parts in this exact arrangement. That's okay! Puberty can be different when that's the case, though.

STAGES OF PUBERTY

On average, puberty begins for most people between the ages of eight and fourteen. It usually starts earlier for people with a vagina than for people with a penis. No matter when puberty starts, most people are all done by their mid-twenties.

FOR EVERY BODY

Body size and shape changes: During puberty, people start to become taller, muscle mass increases and bodies change shape. Sometimes this happens a lot all at once, and that's called a growth spurt. It's normal to gain weight (and to be eating a lot!), and to feel out of proportion. You might even feel like a lumpy potato, because sometimes things that will go somewhere else eventually don't seem to be in the right place on your body right now. This too shall pass.

Skin changes: It's normal for skin to become oilier and bumpier. Pimples show up on the scene. Sweat and body odor usually become stronger.

Body hair: Pubic hair — that's hair around the vulva, the base of the penis, anus, butt or thighs — is usually the first darker, thicker body hair to crop up. It continues growing through puberty. Hair in the armpits usually follows, then chest and facial hair if you're going to get those.

Feeling more sexual: During puberty, most people start to have more sexual feelings and desires than they did before.

13

IF YOU'VE GOT A VAGINA

Breast development: Most often, the first part of puberty is initial breast growth. It's called "breast budding" because growth starts with small lumps under the nipples. Breast development includes changes in the size and shape of the areolas, or nipple areas, as well as the rest of the breasts.

Vaginal discharge: At or around the same time as breast budding, vaginal discharges start showing up. As a person gets older, it's common to become far more aware of what's going on down there.

Genital changes: The inner and outer labia gradually get bigger during puberty, so how the vulva looks can change. Inside the body, the uterus is also growing in size, and the vagina is getting longer.

Menarche: A couple years after breast budding, the menstrual cycle usually begins. It starts first with ovulation, which you can't feel or see. It usually follows a couple weeks later with a first menstrual period, called menarche. A period is what happens when the uterus sheds its lining, usually at the end of each fertility cycle. Periods are made of that lining, blood and other fluids, and come out through the vagina.

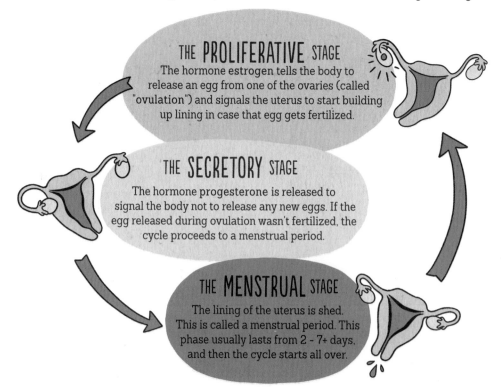

THE **PROLIFERATIVE** STAGE
The hormone estrogen tells the body to release an egg from one of the ovaries (called "ovulation") and signals the uterus to start building up lining in case that egg gets fertilized.

THE **SECRETORY** STAGE
The hormone progesterone is released to signal the body not to release any new eggs. If the egg released during ovulation wasn't fertilized, the cycle proceeds to a menstrual period.

THE **MENSTRUAL** STAGE
The lining of the uterus is shed. This is called a menstrual period. This phase usually lasts from 2 - 7+ days, and then the cycle starts all over.

IF YOU'VE GOT A PENIS

Penis and testicles: Puberty usually starts with testicular (balls) growth. During puberty, the penis and testes will grow to their adult size. Growth of the penis and testicles often aren't finished until the end of puberty.

Erections: Erections are what happens when the blood vessels of the penis fill up with blood and the penis becomes harder and less bendy. Some people call them hard-ons or boners. During puberty, they can happen a lot. Many people get erections several times a day or more. That might feel embarrassing, but it's normal. Erections are usually outside anyone's control.

Ejaculation: That's a word used to describe when the penis releases a cloudy, white fluid called semen. That's something that mostly only happens with masturbation or sex with someone else. When the ability to ejaculate starts, though, it's typical to have "wet dreams." Wet dreams are ejaculation that happens during sleep, for a bunch of possible reasons, like the nervous system just doing its thing, sexual dreams, stimulation from sheets and blankets, or even just having to pee.

Voice changes: During puberty, the voice deepens and can go through stages of being and feeling all over the place, cracking or croaking.

I've got three full hairs on my balls!

SOME PEOPLE ACT LIKE WHEN YOU
GO THROUGH PUBERTY, YOU ARE SUDDENLY AN ADULT.

You are a man or a woman if and when that is what you feel like and what you want to call yourself. Assigning that to people without them deciding for themselves doesn't really work. For example, some people think that you are a woman when you get your period. Some women get their period when they're 10, some do when they're 20. Some never will. Some used to, but don't anymore. Some people who get periods don't feel like women or grown-ups. Some people who don't get periods do feel like women or grown-ups.

THESE THINGS

DON'T ACTUALLY MEAN VERY MUCH ABOUT GROWING UP.

OHHH YEAH, REAL MATURE!

If puberty doesn't mean you're grown up or mature, then what does? When people talk about maturity in that way, what they usually mean is emotional maturity. That's basically people being able to react to things that might feel weird, hard or uncomfortable without freaking out or being jerks.

WHAT DOES MATURITY MEAN TO YOU?

Apologizing and taking responsibility when you do something bad or make a mistake.

Not stealing or cheating on tests or in sports. Not breaking trust that people have in you.

Being honest instead of lying, even when the truth might get you in trouble or make you look bad.

Not being mean or teasing people. Thinking about other people's feelings and trying not to hurt them.

Just don't be a jerk! It's really just about not being a jerk.

PEOPLE USED TO THINK A LOT OF STRANGE THINGS ABOUT

MASTURBATION!

BUT **NONE** OF THIS IS **TRUE!**

MASTURBATION IS HEALTHY,
AND NOTHING TO BE ASHAMED OF.

Masturbation is a word we use to describe when someone touches their own body to give themselves comfort and pleasure, or to express or explore sexual feelings. It's sex by yourself. Usually masturbation involves touching your genitals in some way, but it doesn't have to. It's something that almost everybody has done, and something people usually first did when they were little kids, way before they knew the word for it.

WHY DO PEOPLE MASTURBATE?

For the most part, people masturbate because it feels good. People masturbate to learn about and feel connected to their body and their sexuality. People masturbate because they have sexual feelings and want to express them, or to get relief from feelings of tension. Masturbation is sometimes about having an orgasm and sometimes just about tingly feelings.

The biggest difference between sex with other people and sex with yourself is you're only thinking about your own pleasure and what you want. To be ready for this kind of sex, you just need to be ready to be sexual with yourself.

WEIRD GENITALS!

WORRIED YOUR GENITALS LOOK WEIRD?

FEELING LIKE OTHER PEOPLE'S DO???

You're probably right. In a lot of ways, genitals ARE weird, but that's okay.

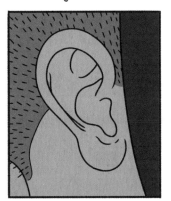

Ears are weird — seriously, look at them.

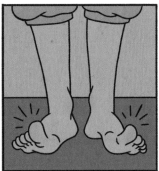

Toes are kind of weird.

Why do we have little fingers on our feet, anyway?

Genitals don't really involve the kinds of bone structure that give other body parts more uniform lines, or the kinds of smooth texture or tone we usually have on other kinds of skin on our bodies. Subtle, unique and sometimes unpredictable things like hormones also influence how they look more than they do other body parts. Because of those things and more, genitals look more free-flowing and just plain different than other body parts do. One set of genitals can look really different from another, even if they are the same "kind" of genitals.

In a lot of ways, they are weird. But it's okay to be weird!

Yeah but... MINE are abnormal. MINE are weird.

I doubt it. Does anything hurt?

No....

If nothing hurts, it's probably fine! Genitals are all different and special in their own way, so you're all good!

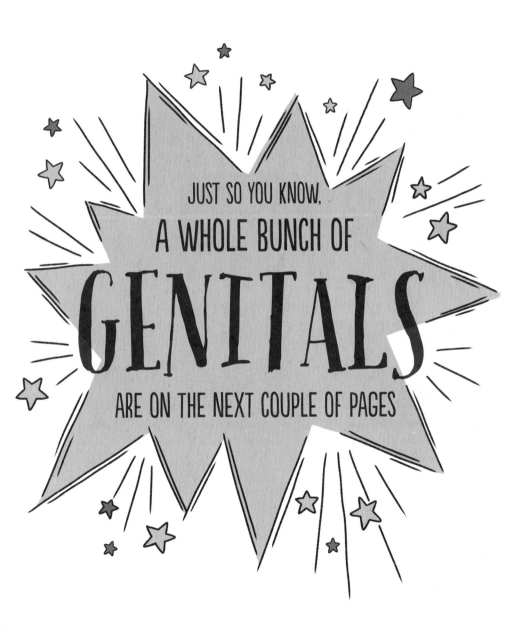

JUST SO YOU KNOW,

A WHOLE BUNCH OF

GENITALS

ARE ON THE NEXT COUPLE OF PAGES

If you don't feel comfortable looking at them right now or yet,
it's okay! Just skip ahead two pages!

GENITALS COME IN ALL SORTS OF DIFFERENT
SIZES, SHAPES AND COLORS

MOST GENITALS ARE LOPSIDED. DRAW THE SECOND HALF OF THE DOODLES BELOW!

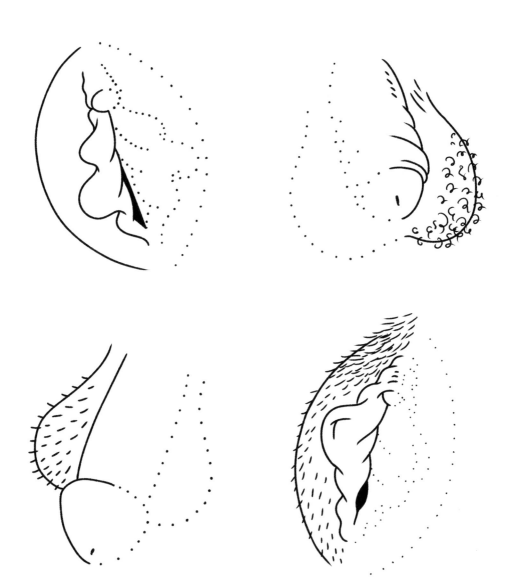

BOYS vs. GIRLS

WHEN IT COMES TO SEX AND SEXUALITY, A LOT OF PEOPLE THINK THAT CERTAIN GROUPS OF PEOPLE ARE SO DIFFERENT, THEY MAY AS WELL BE TOTALLY DIFFERENT SPECIES.

We know from many years of studying human sexuality that people are more the same sexually than different. That's true whether we're talking guys and girls, people with penises and people with vaginas, young people or old people, or people who like the music their parents listen to and people who DO NOT UNDERSTAND WHAT THEY DID TO DESERVE SUCH HIDEOUS TORTURE!

PINK is just a color.

ACTION FIGURES and *dolls* are the same thing.

and SPORTS are for everyone.

The ways people think about what boys are supposed to do or be and what girls are supposed to do or be are usually about a lot of stuff that has nothing to do with who you actually are. Some people feel like both a boy and a girl. Some feel like a girl some days and a boy on other days. Others feel they're neither boys nor girls. (Non-binary is a word some people who feel those ways use to describe themselves.) Whether you're a boy, girl or someone else entirely, your ideas about what you want to do and who you are are the ideas that matter most.

*Gender is basically our own internal sense — not what anyone else thinks or says about it, but how *we* feel — of being a girl, a boy, both or neither and the unique ways we feel like or express those feelings. For more definitions of terms we use in this book, check out the glossary in the back!

You know it's not okay to take my stuff without asking me first, Max.

Sibling fail! Sorry, Yoshimi.

Max always takes this when they want to show their "girly side."

For some people, gender feels like it does for Max. Some parts of them feel girl-like. Some parts feel boy-like.

Other people go back and forth, or feel like both at the same time. Some don't feel like either. Some people don't relate to or feel masculinity or femininity at all. Other people always and only feel like boys or men, or like girls or women.

I don't feel like I have a "boy-side" or like I have "sides" at all. All my sides feel girly.

There's nothing right or wrong about how Max experiences gender, how I do or how girls like Malia or Alexis do.

All those ways are right ways, because they all feel right to each of us!

There's nothing more right or real about how Alexis and Malia are girls than how I am, just because when they were born a doctor said they were girls, and when I was born, a doctor said I was a boy.

Trans girls like me — whose sense of gender isn't the same as the sex a doctor said I was when I was born, that's all — are just as real as girls like Alexis and Malia. That's also true about trans boys.

All three of us are girls because that's how we all feel and that's what we all say we are. Max is...well, whoever Max is today, because that's what they say.

WHAT IS A

When people talk about a crush, they usually mean a strong interest in, or attraction to, someone they're not already in an intimate relationship with. Sometimes crushes are sexual. Sometimes they're not. Sometimes a crush is one-sided. Other times they're mutual. People also use that word because crushes often aren't mutual. That can leave the person who has those feelings feeling pretty crushed for a bit.

MY CRUSH

Crushes can feel intense, even scary!

You might feel scared your crush will find out how you feel.

Or scared they don't like you back!

You might worry your crush, their friends or even your friends will make fun of you. You might worry no one you have a crush on will ever, ever have a crush on you back.

But try not to worry about that too much.

You're great! Someday someone is going to see how great you are and have a crush on you, too. Someone might even be crushing on you already without you knowing it.

I've had a lot of crushes! This is what I've learned:

Respect your crush's personal boundaries, no matter what. Give them space.

Hi! OMG HEYYY I LiKE YOUR HAIR HEY WHAT ARE Y... WANT TO HANG OUT LATER Hi Hi Hi GOING ON

Your crush isn't flawless, even if you think so. Your crush also isn't property or territory for you or anyone else to claim. They're their own person.

It's okay to talk about your crush to your friends. Having a crush can feel embarrassing, but it's nothing to be ashamed of.

It can hurt if your crush isn't crushing on you, but it will be okay. Every crush — even if it doesn't feel like it — will pass in time. No one crushes forever.

If your crush doesn't like you back, don't take it too personally. Whether or not someone likes you back is usually more about them than you.

Having a crush might make you feel uncomfortable, and you may even find yourself acting like a real jerk because of that discomfort. Cut that out! Making someone else feel bad won't make you feel better and it isn't okay.

It may seem like everyone is crushing on someone sometimes. It's not weird if you're not.

HAVE YOU EVER HAD A CRUSH?

Yes.

Many. My current crush turned into a great friendship. It isn't exactly what I wanted in the beginning, but it turns out I'm happy and grateful to have her in my life this way, too.

Yeaaaahhhhh... I'm really lucky she likes me too.

I used to have a big crush on my teacher. I felt weird about it, but I know now it's common to crush on people we look up to. Sometimes we get crushes on people where pursuing those feelings just wouldn't be appropriate or okay. It sucks, but I got over it.

I did, but it was basketball tryouts. So.

DO YOU REALLY WANT TO BE SOMEONE'S
PARTNER, GIRLFRIEND OR BOYFRIEND?

☐ YES
☐ NO
☒ What does that even mean?!

SOMETIMES PEOPLE IN A RELATIONSHIP HAVE RADICALLY DIFFERENT EXPERIENCES IN, AND IDEAS ABOUT, THE RELATIONSHIP THEY'RE IN.

SO, HOW DO YOU FEEL ABOUT BEING SOMEONE'S BOYFRIEND, GIRLFRIEND OR PARTNER?

PROMISES AND Dating

Hold up — dating is the same as being boyfriends, girlfriends or partners, right?

Sometimes, but often not! Dating is just about hanging out to find out what it's like to maybe be together in a certain way.

It's about finding out how you feel more than deciding.

You can go on dates with someone without being in a serious relationship with them yet. That's a great way to figure out if you even want that kind of relationship together!

DATE IDEAS

Watch movie
Board games
Roller skating
Youtube Karaoke
baking
Museum
Videogames

But what about promises? If someone says they'll love you forever but then they break up with you the next day....

We're too young to keep most big promises! These kinds of feelings and relationships are brand new. We can't really know what we'll want or be able to do later.

Feeling like we might love someone forever isn't a promise to be with them forever. "Forever" was probably how someone felt in the moment. That's cool, but no one can promise forevers.

AS IF THERE WAS ONLY ONE *PATH!*

IT'S OKAY TO GO

Some people think if someone leaves a relationship or situation with someone who wants them to stay, they're being a bad person. That's not true. It's okay to go away from places, people, things or relationships that don't feel good, safe or right for us. That's how we find the things that DO feel right and how we protect ourselves or get away from things that can hurt us or others.

IT'S OKAY TO GO IF YOU FEEL UNSAFE.

IT'S OKAY TO GO IF YOU ARE UNHAPPY.

IT'S OKAY TO GO FOR NO REASON AT ALL, YOU JUST AREN'T FEELING IT ANYMORE.

NO ONE WINS FOR STAYING THE LONGEST IN SOMETHING THAT SUCKS.

NO MATTER WHAT, IT'S FINE TO GO WHEN YOU WANT TO GO.

BY *invitation* ONLY

When someone wants you to come to their party, what do they do? They give you an invitation.

YOU'RE INVITED!

PARTY?

Okay, but something like kissing someone, asking someone to go out with you or asking someone to be sexual with you usually isn't going to involve a paper invitation and an RSVP.

OF COURSE NOT, but it should go basically the same way: someone extends an invitation — like

"I really want to kiss you. Can I kiss you?"

"Can I tell my friends that you're my girlfriend?"

or "Do you want to take off your shirt?"

Questions like this give you the most basic information about what they're asking for.

Then you get to accept or decline. But the conversation doesn't need to stop there! You can talk about it more! You can get more specific about what you want or need, or about how you want to do something. You or someone else can also ask for extra things.

IT WOULDN'T BE OKAY TO JUST DRAG SOMEONE TO A PARTY WITHOUT ASKING OR TELLING THEM ANYTHING ABOUT WHAT IT IS, OR CHECKING IF THEY EVEN WANT TO GO.

SAME HERE.

CONSENT WORD SEARCH

Giving invitations and accepting or declining invitations is what people mean when they talk about sexual (and other kinds of!) consent. There are a lot of different ways for people to respond to invitations. In the word search below there are words and phrases that are a yes or a no. Spaces between words have been removed. Circle the words and phrases that mean yes and strike through the words and phrases that mean no.

```
          R E M W                    Z K N G
        S Q W A W B                J K J C F R
      N O W A Y D W K            S Y Z D N O I G
    O C Y O Q R Q A W W O    O T K R H F Z J E
  A G C O R S N R T H A T    F E E L S G O O D Z
L R Q B R B V L X Y N O T    N O W B Y I P P E E M
N G I Z O V T A K X N X W    G Q Y O U C A N X N P
I M E X C I T E D M F L S    T O P Q J V F R P L R
E L S Y D F P A C I M R E    A D Y L O V E T H I S
Q A E T C U A O K K O O A    Z H O M D Y I C C W L
T K E P S W M F G Y U C C    K A V E K B K J L S Z
A U M M M Q X X W S P W Z    D T O X V L F K J
U H B C E X N N P L E A S    E D O N T R H N I
  W E P F T N M A Y B E      C P H I Q L S I C
    W Z N O C N O T L I K    E T H A T I Z
      C J D Y Q I D O N T    K N O W Q T
        K G D U D I B L N    Y E S Q P
          O U L R S M O R    E K A D
            A N O P E Z G    U Z R
              N U B R N L    N M
              Q V C A C P
                O W Q L
                A P
```

THERE MIGHT HAVE BEEN A COUPLE IN THERE WHERE YOU WEREN'T SURE.

If someone ever says something where you aren't sure if it's a yes or a no, you just ask more questions to find out.

IT'S NOT SEX, IT'S JUST MESSING AROUND

When some people say "sex" or "have sex," they only mean the kind of sex — called vaginal intercourse — where people interlock a penis and a vagina. But that's not the only way for people to have sex, or be sexual. Not everyone knows or understands that, though. And some people only call it sex if it can make a baby.

WHY DO PEOPLE HAVE SEX TOGETHER?

Most of the time, when people choose to masturbate, they do it to explore and enjoy feelings of pleasure. People are often curious about what their own sexuality is like, and they like finding out more about it and themselves. When people choose to be sexual with other people, it's often for the same reasons, but multiplied. People are usually looking to experience the ways another person can make sex feel different, both physically and emotionally.

That's how I feel about rollerskating! I love to go by myself and skate alone.

I don't need anyone else to skate with me in order to want and enjoy it, but sometimes going with another person is really fun in a different way than skating alone is.

Yeah! I love dancing by myself. But when I'm dancing with someone else, I enjoy that person being there and dancing with them. We come up with moves together I wouldn't by myself!

I think sex is like that stuff... but like, seriously next level.

Of course, one kind of sex (vaginal intercourse) can create pregnancies, which can create whole new people. That's not the most common reason people have that kind of sex, but that's one other reason people can choose to have sex sometimes.

SO WHAT'S THE DIFFERENCE BETWEEN SEX AND "MESSING AROUND"?

It's not like there's "Messing Around" and "The Big Sex" with no crossover. Or like one is no big deal and the other is THE big deal. It depends.

Messing around doesn't always feel like no big deal, even though it sounds like that. Messing around and "the big sex" can both be huge. Or not.

Sex with someone else is when both people are expressing their sexual feelings and wants with their bodies, and when both people feel it's sex.

On the other hand, just because someone does something sexual, that also doesn't necessarily mean they "HAD SEX" in the way a lot of people mean.

Just remember, different kinds of sex come with different risks, so if you do decide you're ready, make sure to do your homework first!

IF IT WASN'T A CHOICE

If it wasn't a choice for everybody, then it wasn't sex for everybody. Sex is about *choosing* to be sexual. When a person does something sexual to someone else without their permission, or against their will, it's not sex. It's sexual abuse or assault. Sex is about sharing, not tricking or stealing. It's stealing if somebody takes something without asking, without the other person saying yes or makes someone say yes when they didn't want to. It's sharing if the other person offers or gladly shares if someone else asks.

STEALING

Taking something without asking.

STEALING

Asking, but taking that thing anyway when the answer is no.

STEALING

Tricking or talking someone into giving you that thing.

SHARING!

Asking, and accepting that thing when the answer is yes.

HOW DO YOU KNOW WHEN YOU'RE READY FOR SEX STUFF??

To be ready for sex, we need to have a realistic idea of what can happen, before, during and after. We need access to the things we need to be sexual in a way that's safe for everybody involved. If we have these things, and we feel ready, we probably are. But many people in their early teens don't feel ready and don't have that access.

This graph only counts certain types of sex in one country, but you get the general picture!

PERCENTAGE OF YOUNG PEOPLE WHO HAVE HAD SEXUAL INTERCOURSE, BY AGE

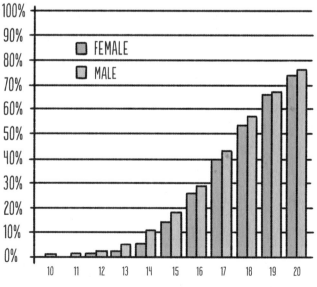

☐ FEMALE
☐ MALE

Graph adapted from the Guttmacher Institute in 2017. All survey participants in the United States.

WHAT'S IT MEAN TO BE READY FOR SEX WITH SOMEONE?

That's complicated. All the possible experiences we can have vary so much — like what we're doing, with whom, when, where, why and all the many hows. We — the people who can be having those experiences — are all so different, including even from one year to the next, all by ourselves. But there are some very basic things that can help you know if you are ready.

WHEN DO YOU THINK YOU WILL BE READY FOR SEX STUFF?

Uh, when I want to be sexual with a partner in the first place.

When I have access to sexual health information, healthcare and safer sex supplies.

When I have support from caring people I trust.

When my future love and I have respect and trust for each other!

When we both understand consent, like how to ask each other what we do and don't want to do.

Some other things to consider would be: a shared want to be really intimate with each other, being comfortable being naked with someone else, emotional maturity to handle some really intimate and even embarrassing things together, a real understanding of the risks involved, knowing how to reduce them and being okay taking them, and the whole idea of all this not really freaking you out!

WHY IS *sex* SUCH A BIG DEAL?

Sometimes it's a big deal. Sometimes it isn't. Or it is a big deal, but it doesn't feel like one. In some basic ways. though, it is always at least *kind of* a big deal. Any way of being sexual with someone else presents a bunch of things that usually make at least one person involved vulnerable. That, all by itself, is a very big deal.

Well, I know I'll be ready!

Come on, Rico, you don't know that.

Most things people call sex — like oral sex or intercourse — come with a lot of risks and responsibilities.

Most people who are 11, 13 or even 15 probably aren't going to be able to manage, or even want to try to manage all of that!

I mean, yeah, pregnancy could be a risk....

Or hurting someone's feelings!

ARE YOU...

GAY? **Straight?** **BOTH?** **Neither?**

Ugh! People make it like there's only two options, and two kinds of people: gay or straight.

But there are waaaay more than those two kinds of people, and waaaay more choices about that part of being a person than two!

It often seems like people are either gay or straight, but this just isn't true! Loads of people fall somewhere in the middle, on the outside or feel different about this altogether.

Saying there are only gay people and straight people is like saying that there are only cat people and dog people.

SEXUAL ORIENTATION
CROSSWORD

These are some words that people can use, defined in ways they're most often used. But it's important to remember that even if someone seems to fit one of these words, we shouldn't put them on them without their permission. Each of us gets to decide what, if any, words we use to describe our identity. We also get to have our own unique definitions for our own identity words!

SEXUAL ORIENTATION WORD BANK

Gay	Ambisexual	Lesbian
Heterosexual	Questioning	Pansexual
Homosexual	Straight	Asexual
Demisexual	Bisexual	Gynesexual
Androsexual	Queer	(If you get stuck, try checking the glossary in the back of the book!)

SEXUAL ORIENTATION CROSSWORD

ACROSS

2. A short word that describes being only or mostly attracted to people of a different gender than yourself.
7. A word for someone who can feel attraction to people of all gender identities, or who doesn't experience gender as a major factor in their attractions, period.
8. A word for trying to figure out your orientation or just not knowing what it is right now.
9. A formal word that describes being only or mostly attracted to people of a different gender than yourself.
10. A term that describes not feeling any sexual attraction to other people, or having those feelings but no desire to act on them in a sexual way.
11. A word for being attracted to people of more than one gender.
12. Being attracted to both masculinity and femininity, to either, or experiencing gender as a non-issue in attraction to other people.
14. Being only or mostly attracted to masculinity.

DOWN

1. A word for a woman who is only or mostly attracted to other women.
3. A formal word that describes being only or mostly attracted to people of the same or similar gender as yourself.
4. Being only or mostly attracted to femininity.
5. A word to describe someone who doesn't feel sexual attraction unless some kind of emotional bond is formed first. It's considered part of the asexual spectrum.
6. A word often used to describe sexual orientations or gender identities that may fall outside of heterosexuality or gendernormativity. Some people also use it instead of pansexual, ambisexual or bisexual.
13. A short word that describes a man who is only or mostly attracted to other men OR someone who is only or mostly attracted to people of their same or similar gender.

SEXUAL IDENTITY
ISN'T A LIFELONG COMMITMENT

I've tried on a few different ways of identifying now, but almost everyone treated me like that's how I had to be forever, even though my feelings changed a lot.

In 4th grade I gave a valentine to Jessica Thompson and my friends were all in a tizzy.

The next year I gave one to Sam, and we all remember how confused everyone was.

In 6th grade I got a chocolate heart from Tyler M.

Last year I realized Valentine's Day just exists for the candy companies and boycotted the whole thing.

BE MINE

but...

It's like how people ask you what you want to be when you grow up. I've already run through so many answers to that question.

Plus, no one has to choose to be just one thing in the first place!

I'm so tired of feeling like I have to **label myself!**

Um, I don't feel like I have to label myself.

It's a choice, and I like having shorthand I can use to describe myself.

Right now I call myself gay, because I've only ever had crushes on girls.

That doesn't mean I'll always have to use that word, or only ever like girls, but that's okay.

If my feelings change, my words can change.

I like having that word because it makes me feel validated in my identity.

It reminds me that other people are and have always been like me, too, so I don't feel alone.

QUEER HISTORY

It gives me a way to describe something personal and private about myself without having to tell my whole life story.

You can't be a fortune teller and know what the future holds.

You can only know what you're interested in and have feels about up to now. A word or phrase you use for yourself today isn't a promise to be one thing forever and ever, or even next week.

I still don't like labels.

I still do.

55

ARE YOU GAY? STRAIGHT? BOTH? NEITHER? WHO EVEN KNOWS?

WHAT DO YOU THINK? HERE'S SOME SPACE TO WRITE YOUR OWN THOUGHTS.

_____
_____
_____
_____
_____
_____
_____

WHAT DOES IT MEAN TO BE A VIRGIN?

Speaking of words, do you guys know what the word "virgin" means? Some older kids were saying things to my sister about it, and she was really upset.

I know! I looked it up when I was reading a fantasy book because a "virgin" was being sacrificed to a dragon, and I didn't know what it meant, either.

It means "a person who has never had sexual intercourse."

Your sister must have had sex.

That's why they were being mean to her? I don't get —

57

GAH! **I HATE THAT WORD!**

When someone calls themselves a "virgin,"

it usually just means they haven't chosen to do whatever it is they consider sex with someone else yet.

When they say they're not one, that usually means they did choose to be sexual with someone.

When people say someone else is or isn't a virgin, they are usually being mean or judgy, and often suggesting that sex itself is wrong.

But people who have sex and people who don't have sex are equally good! Some people don't get that.

No one is a different person, a better person or a worse person if they have had sex before, whatever their reasons or circumstances.

A NOTE ABOUT DOUBLE STANDARDS

Usually virginity has been and is still only really about girls and women. It's not usually about boys or men. Nobody usually says they're not as good if *they're* not virgins. This can even get dangerous. People have been abused in very serious ways around the idea of virginity.

A lot of the -isms and other kinds of bias in our world — like sexism or racism — set up double standards. A double standard is where people from one group (a more privileged one) are given more freedom to do certain things or act certain ways than another group of people (one or more with less privilege). For example, men have more power than women and non-binary people in the world, so there are lots of double standards that benefit men most, and make sure they keep most of the power. One double standard like this is that in most cultures, it's not that big of a deal if men have sex with a bunch of women, but if women have sex with a bunch of men, it's a totally different story.

One last thing: You know how sometimes people say someone can't be in their group so they can get themselves some power and make that other person feel like an outsider? People sometimes do that around people and sex, or even just their ideas about someone and sex. They say something — sometimes that something isn't even true — in order to push them out.

You can't sit with us!!!!

We can't know anything about anyone's sexuality, sex life, or body parts unless that person chooses to tell us.

We also can't know what a person's sexuality, sex life, or body parts or anything else means about or to that person, if anything, unless THEY tell us.

My sexual identity, history or beliefs also don't determine my worth. Being queer or not, having had sex or not? Nothing like that makes me a better or a worse person.

And look: if words that talk about your sex life, like virgin, are words you want to use for yourself, you get to, and you get to decide what they mean. What's not cool is putting them on someone else.

And what's REALLY not cool is to call people those things to make someone feel bad, ashamed or excluded.

YEAH!

ASSEMBLE YOUR SUPERTEAM!

My mom told me that!

You talk to your mom about this stuff?

Well yeah, she's part of my Superteam.

One of the easiest ways to wind up in a real mess when it comes to things like dating or sex stuff is to do it in total secret, without letting other people who care about you in on what's going on. All of this goes a lot better with support and with honest, caring feedback. One of the most important things you can do for yourself is to make and keep a team of people in your life you can talk to about these kinds of things, and who are there for you for support or help.

YOU

My Superteam is going to be our example! Here are some very important roles to fill for your team. Maybe seeing who's on my team will give you ideas for your own.

You're the hero of the story. The main man, the leading lady, the valiant gender non-specific champion of teen years, the Weird Platypus-About-Town. You are facing some of your greatest challenges yet! You are ready to join forces to take on things too big for any one hero to tackle. **Who will stand at your side?**

YOUR SIDEKICK

That's me!

Your sidekick is probably a best friend. You can tell them almost anything and trust them to be cool with you. No matter what, they'll always come around and you know they'll have your back. This is the person you can tell ANYTHING TO! (Or close to anything.) This person will always be there for you when you really need them, and vice-versa. If someone is your sidekick, you're probably their sidekick, too.

YOUR PARENTAL FIGURE

Your parental figure or figures have power, privilege and experience you don't. They can do some of the heavy lifting if you are out of your depth. It might not always be easy to tell them everything, but even with the rough stuff, they're going to love and care for you and they always want to help you work it out.

I don't really talk to my parents about much, but my big sister Sonia is always around to help me out.

It's okay if you don't have people to fill all of these roles. Your team can even be just you and your dog or your journal, for now. The older you get, the easier it usually becomes to grow your team.

YOUR MENTOR

Your mentor teaches you a lot about life (think of them as your Jedi master). Your mentor could be a teacher, a neighbor, a coach, a counselor or any adult that you respect. Your mentor might not be in your life as often as other people. You might not even tell them a whole lot a lot of the time, but they're always dropping some serious knowledge and would be there for you if you asked.

My guitar teacher Roy is really cool. I only see him once a week for lessons, but he's taught me a lot about life, not just guitar.

YOUR LEAGUE

Think of your league like your band. Sometimes you all play together. Sometimes you choose to jam with only one or two of them. It's your league, for you, and you get to pick who you want to talk to, and about what, based on what you want and need, and what each of them are good at. Everyone may not always have the answer, but you are going to figure it out together.

My league is made up of my friends!

Someone you're going out with can be part of your team. After all, hopefully that's someone who cares about you and who you trust. But not JUST that person, especially since you need people you can talk to about that person and that relationship.

FIND ALL THE PEOPLE YOU COULD MAYBE TALK TO!

```
W  J  Q  M  S  G  D  S  N  U  R  S  E  O  V  S
F  G  W  Y  P  G  O  O  I  Q  Z  S  K  W  C  J
K  I  Q  S  Y  C  C  T  M  T  G  C  O  I  T  T
U  P  Y  G  Y  G  T  L  K  L  I  H  O  C  W  Y
W  X  O  L  K  R  O  N  N  Q  D  O  W  O  P  U
I  S  P  J  L  U  R  S  E  G  F  O  Q  A  A  G
S  I  B  L  I  N  G  K  J  S  A  L  J  C  R  R
Y  S  Z  I  B  M  W  Q  M  R  Y  C  Q  H  E  A
Z  T  H  E  R  A  P  I  S  T  M  O  D  T  N  N
B  F  F  A  A  R  E  J  E  C  W  U  X  T  T  D
C  S  G  G  R  E  H  F  R  I  E  N  D  E  Z  P
P  U  V  D  I  Y  L  E  D  O  Q  S  Z  A  G  A
N  D  X  R  A  B  L  J  V  L  Y  E  T  C  R  R
W  W  Z  H  N  D  R  W  G  X  E  L  J  H  R  E
B  U  D  G  X  S  G  K  J  A  F  O  P  E  Y  N
S  S  P  X  I  Q  H  I  R  U  P  R  E  R  U  T
```

Teacher
Coach
Parent
Friend
BFF
Librarian
Doctor
Nurse
Therapist
School Counselor
Grandparent
Sibling

and many, many more!

KNOW YOUR COMMUNITY RESOURCES!

Depending on where you live, there are most likely resources available to you for all kinds of support or help. Is there a clinic nearby? Does your school have a school nurse or a guidance counselor? How about a library? Even if there are no organizations or community centers right where you're at, there are many online resources that could be super helpful to you! Try searching through the internet and see what you find.

WHO IS ON YOUR
SUPERTEAM?

Here's a page for you to write down your own Superteam! You can fill it out here in the book, or you can make a copy and use that instead. If you don't have someone for every category, that's okay, and you can put more than one person in any category you want!

YOU:

YOUR SIDEKICK(S):

YOUR PARENTAL FIGURE(S):

YOUR MENTOR(S):

YOUR LEAGUE:

ANY OTHER PEOPLE, ORGANIZATIONS OR RESOURCES:

IN CONCLUSION

WHAT IS ONE LAST THING YOU WANT TO LEAVE EVERYONE WITH?

You can be a studmuffin without being a jerk.

Don't let somebody else tell you who you are. If you don't know yet, nobody gets to rush you.

All you need is love... and respect and communication and your friends and personal interests.... but mostly love!

Even if you feel really different from everyone else, you're probably not alone.

Just do you.

Dear you,

The friends in this book are pretty fantastic. We hope you have at least one or two friends like Malia, Rico, Max, Sam or Alexis in your life — and that you're that kind of friend yourself! We hope you feel as safe with and supported by your friends as they do. That's how friends should feel with each other, even with touchy subjects like sex and bodies.

But we know that sometimes good friends can be hard to come by. And even when you have good friends, things can go sideways, especially at this time of life. Friends might act really weird out of nowhere, even if they've always been pretty awesome.

In case your friends or others in your life aren't acting anything like the ones in this book, we're really sorry. We know how badly that can hurt and how scary and lonely that can feel, especially when the not-great stuff is happening around sensitive things like bodies, sexuality or gender.

If that's how it is for you right now, we want to make sure you know that you deserve good, safe friends and other people around you who are kind. If you don't have those right now, that's not because there's something wrong with you or because you aren't worthy. **You are worthy, and nothing is wrong with you**: life and people are just tough and prickly sometimes. Sometimes they're even harder than that. We hope you'll take a look at your Superteam, and that you can find and pick at least one person on it to talk to and connect with. Help services that Scarleteen and other organizations offer can also give you support and company, and even fill one of those Superteam roles, too. You don't ever have to be without a friend in any of this, even at times when there don't seem to be friends to be found.

With love,
Heather and Isabella

GLOSSARY

Ambisexual: A word for being attracted to both or either masculinity and femininity, or experiencing gender as a non-issue in attraction to other people.

Androsexual: Being only or mostly attracted to masculinity.

Asexual: A word usually used to describe either just not feeling sexual attraction to other people, or having those feelings, but not feeling the desire to act on on them in a sexual way.

Bisexual: A word for being attracted to people of more than one gender. Ambisexual, pansexual or queer are other words some people use for this.

Boundaries: Emotional, physical or other kinds of limits we set, or lines we draw, with other people.

Cisgender: A word for people who feel like their gender identity "matches" the sex they were assigned at birth.

Consent: To agree to do something or give permission. In the context of sex, consenting or active consent is about the process of everyone involved clearly asking for permission, responding to each other and respecting each other's answers.

Demisexual: A word to describe someone who doesn't feel sexual attraction unless some kind of emotional bond is formed first. It's considered part of the asexual spectrum.

Gay: A short word that can mean a man who is only or mostly attracted to other men OR someone who is only or mostly attracted to people of their same or similar gender. *Homosexual* is a formal word for this.

Gender: Our own internal sense of being a boy, a girl, both or neither, and the unique ways we experience and express those feelings.

Gender nonconforming and Gendernormative: Many roles, ways of acting, presenting or otherwise being are considered to be "normal" and "correct" (or not) for certain genders or when it comes to ways of thinking about gender. Gendernormativity is about what's in line with those kinds of common expectations or ideas. Gender nonconforming is about gender expressions or ways of thinking about gender that are different than those "norms."

Transgender or non-binary identities are examples of gender nonconforming identities; being a girl who wants to be a firefighter or a boy who loves makeup are examples of gender nonconforming feelings or behaviors. Cisgender identities are an example of gendernormative identities; being a boy who wants to drive racecars or a girl who loves the color pink are examples of gendernormative feelings or behaviors.

Genitals: The external parts of the the reproductive system, like the vulva, testicles and penis.

Gynesexual: Being only or mostly attracted to femininity.

Heterosexual: A formal word that describes being only or mostly attracted to people of a different gender than yourself. *Straight* is an informal, short word for this.

Homosexual: A formal word that can mean a man who is only or mostly attracted to other men OR someone who is only or mostly attracted to people of their same or similar gender. *Gay* or *lesbian* are shorter, informal words that mean the same thing.

Hormones: Chemical substances produced by the body that control or influence the activity of certain cells, systems or organs. Some hormones that often play a part in sexual development, reproduction or sexuality are estrogen, testosterone, progestin, vasopressin, dopamine, adrenaline, noradrenaline, and FSH, LH and hCG.

Intersex: A word used to describe a person or conditions where someone is born with reproductive or sexual anatomy, or an arrangement of sex chromosomes, that just doesn't fit the way that male or female sex is usually defined. Sometimes people don't know they're intersex until they're in their teens or older. Some common ways of being intersex are Androgen Insensitivity Syndrome, Klinefelter's Syndrome or Adrenal Hyperplasia.

Intimacy: Seeking or having closeness of some kind with someone else. Sometimes people use "intimacy" to mean being sexual with someone else. That's one kind of intimacy, but not the only kind. Some other common ways of being intimate include sharing secrets or tricky feelings, sharing things of great value to us or letting other people take care of us.

Lesbian: A word for a woman who is only or mostly attracted to other women. *Homosexual* is a formal word for this.

Orgasm: A body event that is controlled by and mostly happens in the involuntary nervous system, usually in response to some kind of physical or mental sexual stimulation. Orgasm usually creates muscle contractions in and around the genitals, other muscular spasms throughout the body, and a feeling of relaxation or release. Most people enjoy how orgasm feels. Sometimes people use other words for orgasm, like climax, getting off or come/cum.

Pansexual: A word for someone who can feel attraction to people of all gender identities, or who doesn't experience gender as a major factor in their attractions, period. Sometimes people who feel like this use bisexual, ambisexual or queer, instead.

Pleasure: A feeling of enjoyment or satisfaction, which can include sexual pleasure.

Porn or pornography: Media, like books, photographs or videos, that is created with the aim of arousing sexual feelings in people and that some people use to stimulate or increase sexual feelings in themselves.

Queer: A word often used to describe sexual orientations or gender identities that may fall outside of heterosexuality or gendernormativity. Some people also use it instead of *pansexual, ambisexual* or *bisexual.*

Questioning: A word for trying to figure out your orientation or just not knowing what it is right now.

Relationship: Any kind of ongoing interaction or association with another person, place or thing, like a friendship, family or dating relationship. Sometimes people use the word relationship to only mean a romantic, sexual, "serious" or committed relationship, even though that's not all this word means.

Sex: The word sex can mean two different things.

    1) A way most people are classified at birth, usually either as male or female (even though there are actually more sexes than just those two).

    2) Any number of different things people actively do alone or with other people to explore and express sexual feelings. When people are talking about that second kind of sex, there are also some common words used for some of the common ways people have sex with each other. When people say *sexual intercourse* that usually describes being sexual by putting genitals together, like a penis and vagina. When people put a word in front of sex, like "*oral sex*" or "*manual sex*," that usually means being sexual with whatever body part or action is named (like oral = the mouth, or manual = the hands) and someone else's genitals.

Sexuality: Our experience and expression of parts of ourselves and our lives we feel are about sex for us. That can (but doesn't have to!) include our bodies, their systems and parts, sexual orientation, gender identity, ways we express or explore our sexual feelings alone or with other people, sexual interactions or relationships, and our feelings and thoughts about any of those things and about sex in general.

Sexual assault or abuse: When someone does something that is sexual for them to someone else against their will, without their permission or their wanted, active participation. We also use these words to describe experiencing these kinds of abuse. Sometimes sexual assault or abuse involves physical or other kinds of violence; other times it does not. Sexual violence or rape are other common words for these experiences or actions.

Sexually transmitted infections: Kinds of contagious illness — viruses, parasites or bacteria — that are mostly transmitted through ways people are physically sexual with each other. Some examples of sexually transmitted infections (which are often called STIs or STDs for short) are chlamydia, HIV or HPV.

Sexual identity: How someone thinks of, sees, or defines themselves in terms of their sexuality. That can be as simple as just being about sexual orientation, or as complex as being about all the ways sexuality feels like a part of who someone is or their life.

Sexual orientation: A term — like *homosexual, heterosexual, bisexual, queer, straight, lesbian, gay, asexual* — used to describe a person's usual or current pattern of sexual or emotional attraction to other people in terms of their gender.

Straight: A short word that describes being only or mostly attracted to people of a different gender than yourself. *Heterosexual* is the formal word for this.

Transgender (or trans): A gender identity for someone who doesn't feel like they "match" their assigned sex.

— I CAN'T KEEP UP WITH THE SLANG! —

What does INSERT TERM FOR SEXUAL ACTIVITY HERE mean?

Slang words — informal, vague words that people make up — for sexual activities are tricky. They don't mean the same things to everyone, they change all the time, and half the time, people saying them don't even know what they mean. If and when you're not sure what someone means with a sexual term they are using, you have to ask them. That doesn't mean you're not cool enough to know, by the way. In fact, sometimes people using slang do because THEY are too embarrassed to call things what they are.

page 42 answers:

CONSENT WORD SEARCH

| Green Rectangle = Yes | Red Line = No | Yellow = Not Sure, talk about it more |

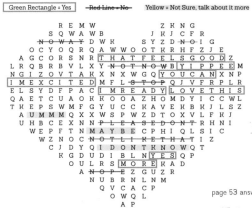

```
                R E M W              Z K N G
              S Q W A W B          J K J C F R
            N O W A Y D W K       S Y Z N O I G
          O C Y O Q R Q A W W O O T K R H F Z J E
        A G C O R S N R T H A T F E E L S G O O D Z
      L R Q B R B V L X Y N O T N O W B Y I P P E E M
    N G I Z O V T A K X N X W G Q Y O U C A N X N P
    I M E X C I T E D M F L S T O P Q J V F R P L R
    E L S Y D F P A C I M R E A D Y L O V E T H I S
    Q A E T C U A O K K O O A Z H O M D Y I C C W L
    T K E P S W M F G Y U C C K A V E K B K J L S Z
    A U M M M Q X X W S P W Z D T O X V L F K J
    U H B C E X N N P L E A S E D O N T R H N I
      W E P F T N M A Y B E C P H I Q L S I C
        W Z N O C N O T L I K E T H A T I Z
        C J D Y Q I D O N T K N O W Q T
        K G D U D I B L N Y E S Q P
          O U L R S M O R E K A D
            A N O P E Z G U Z R
              N U B R N L N M
              Q V C A C P
                O W Q L
                A P
```

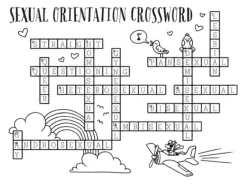

page 53 answers:

SEXUAL ORIENTATION CROSSWORD

page 64 answers:

FIND ALL THE PEOPLE YOU COULD MAYBE TALK TO!

```
W J Q M S G D S N U R S E O V S
F G W Y P G O O I Q Z S K W C J
K I Q S Y C C T M T G C O I T T
U P Y G Y G T L K L I H O C W Y
W X O L K R O N N Q D O W O P U
I S P J L U R S E G F O Q A A G
S I B L I N G K J S A L J C R R
Y S Z I B M W Q M R Y C Q H E A
Z T H E R A P I S T M O D T N N
B F F A A R E J E C W U X T T D
C S G G R E H F R I E N D E Z P
P U V D I Y L E D O Q S Z A G A
N D X R A B L J V L Y E T C R R
W W Z H N D R W G X E L J H R E
B U D G X S G K J A F O P E Y N
S S P X I Q H I R U P R E R U T
```

Teacher
Coach
Parent
Friend
BFF
Librarian
Doctor
Nurse
Therapist
School Counselor
Grandparent
Sibling

and many,
many more!

We are so grateful for:

Tim Rotman, Lauren Gillette, Kelsey Hodgson, Anwar Khuri, Shawn Morgenlander, Amara Leipzig, Ramona Riecke, Alfredo Luna, D'Arcy Mies, Cheyenne McQuain, Colin Bunnell, Troublepants, Sam Wall, Jacob Mirzaian and the rest of the team at Scarleteen, and the good folks of Chicago Cartoonist Crit Club.

The very highest of fives to Liam, Talullah, Alissa, Cat and Vivi, our amazing team of young readers and helpers.

We'd also like to thank Peter Mayle and his winsome and loveable sperm cell from *Where Did I Come From?* for inspiring us both when we were too wee to know the big things that kind of inspiration probably led to.

Last, but most certainly not least, we'd like to thank platypuses everywhere for being as weird as we are.

From Peter Mayle's Where Did I Come From?

HEATHER CORINNA

Heather is a writer, educator, activist and youth advocate, and the founder, designer and director of Scarleteen (www.scarleteen.com), one of the very first sex education websites and services online. They're the author of *S.E.X.: The All-You-Need-To-Know Sexuality Guide to Get You Through Your Teens and Twenties*, and were a contributing writer and editor for the last version of *Our Bodies, Ourselves*. Heather is queer and has had disabilities since they were a kid, is from Chicago, but loves the wilderness, makes music and food every chance they get, walks everywhere with their dog, Troublepants, and can't wait for it to be summer, whatever the time of year.

ISABELLA ROTMAN

Isabella is a cartoonist and illustrator from Maine living in Chicago. Her art is usually about the ocean, feminist mermaids, crushing loneliness, people in the woods, or sex. Isabella is the author of two sexual health comics: *You're So Sexy When You Aren't Transmitting STIs*, and *Not On My Watch; The Bystanders' Handbook for the Prevention of Sexual Violence*. Isabella has been Artist in Residence at Scarleteen since 2013. Isabella might be a sea witch, but don't ask her about it. She's not just giving her secrets away that easily.

LUKE B. HOWARD

Luke is an illustrator, cartoonist and printmaker living in beautiful, sleepy swampy New Orleans, Louisiana. When he's not coloring graphic novels, he makes sci-fi comics about feelings, and an autobiographical zine called *Abandon Ship*. He's been screenprinting artwork for over 10 years, and spends way too much time fussing with ornery Risograph copiers and greasy offset presses. He loves self-publishing, and has helped organize the New Orleans Comics & Zine Fest (NOCAZ) since 2016. If he's not working, tinkering or organizing, he's probably playing D&D with his friends.

MORE COOL THINGS!

Maybe you want to get your hands on even more sex ed, or maybe one part of this book got your attention and you want to learn more about that topic. Here are some books and websites that can help! We may not agree with everything that every resource on this list says, but we strongly feel that each of these books and websites have valuable and helpful things to say about sex, bodies or growing up!

ONLINE:
- **Amaze**: sex, relationships and bodies education videos for kids ages 4 - 14 : www.amaze.org
- **New Moon Girls**: a magazine made for and by girls: www.newmoongirls.com
- **Scarleteen**: the giant and super-amazing sex education resource for young people online (and where Heather and Isabella work!): www.scarleteen.com
- **Sex, Etc.**: another online sex education resource for young people: www.sexetc.org

OTHER BOOKS AND COMICS:
- *Beyond Magenta: Transgender Teens Speak Out* by Susan Kuklin
- *The Boy's Body Book* and *The Girl's Body Book* by Kelli Dunham, RN BSN
- *Celebrate Your Body!* by Sonya Renee Taylor
- *Doing it Right* by Bronwen Pardes
- *Gay and Lesbian History for Kids* by Jerome Pohlen
- *It's Perfectly Normal* and *It's So Amazing!* by Robie H. Harris
- *Queer: A Graphic History* by Meg-John Barker and Julia Scheele
- *A Quick & Easy Guide to They/Them Pronouns* by Archie Bongiovanni and Tristan Jimerson
- *A Quick & Easy Guide to Queer & Trans Identities* by Mady G and J.R. Zuckerberg
- *Sex Is a Funny Word* and *What Makes a Baby?* by Cory Silverberg and Fiona Smythe
- *S.E.X.: The All-You-Need-To-Know Sexuality Guide to Get You Through Your Teens and Twenties* by Heather Corinna

FOR PARENTS AND OTHER ADULTS WHO DON'T WANT TO MESS THIS STUFF UP:
- *Beyond Birds and Bees: Bringing Home a New Message to Our Kids About Sex, Love, and Equality* by Bonnie J. Rough
- *Breaking the Hush Factor* by Dr. Karen Rayne
- *For Goodness Sex* by Al Vernacchio
- *Raising the Transgender Child: A Complete Guide for Parents, Families, and Caregivers* by Michele Angello and Ali Bowman
- Scarleteen Confidential: www.scarleteen.com/tags/scarleteen_confidential
- *This is a Book for Parents of Gay Kids* by Danielle Owens-Reid and Kristin Russo

Read more from Limerence Press

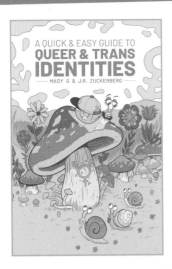

A Quick & Easy Guide to Queer & Trans Identities

By Mady G and J.R. Zuckerberg

Covering essential topics like sexuality, gender identity, coming out, and navigating relationships, this guide explains the spectrum of human experience through informative comics, interviews, worksheets, and imaginative examples.

A Quick & Easy Guide to They/Them Pronouns

By Archie Bongiovanni & Tristan Jimerson

A quick and easy resource for people who use they/them pronouns, and people who want to learn more!

For more information on these and other fine Limerence Press comic books and graphic novels, visit www.onipress.com. To find a comic specialty store in your area, visit www.comicshops.us.